The House of You

Built for a Purpose. Structured for His Plan.

Michelle Renée Chudy

KINGDOM KINETIC
Publishing

Scripture Translations

New International Version

New Living Translation

New King James Version

The House of You

Built for a Purpose. Structured for His Plan.

Text Copyright © 2016 by Michelle R. Chudy

Printed in the United States of America. For information address contact@michellechudy.com

Published by Kingdom Kinetic Publishing
Lexington, Kentucky USA
Book design copyright © 2016 by Kingdom Kinetic Publishing.
All rights reserved.
Cover design by Michelle Chudy
Interior design by Michelle Chudy

Published in the United States of America
ISBN: 978-0-9976989-2-3
1. Nonfiction, Religion, Christian Life, Spiritual Growth
2. Nonfiction, Self-Help, Spiritual

Dedication

To my brothers and sisters in Christ, who journey seeking Him, and only want more...to those who have their heart set on destiny, desire His purpose, want to bring heaven to earth, and are determined to bring glory to His name, this book is dedicated to you.

In Christ,

Michelle

Acknowledgements

A word of thanks to the men and women of God whom He used to fill me. To even the ones who were not of Him, but contributed to life experiences that allowed me to glean His wisdom by eating the meat and spitting out the bones – a recent gem of a quote borrowed from a new and dear friend!

To all the people who have shared their heart, hopes and wounds with me, and allowed me to gain knowledge, insight and understanding while helping them on their journey.

And a very generous thank you and big hug to my editor for your reviews, critiques and very polite edits. Not only are you a blessing, your night-owl ways positioned you to be a ready asset for this kingdom assignment. You are a magnificent gift from Jesus Himself!

Table of Contents

Introduction

Have you ever been in a shoddy house that fools you with its appearance because it's pleasing to the eye? The curb appeal lures you into believing that it's worth so much more. The exterior trim and treatments scream high class. You can't wait to take a look inside, and are sure it won't disappoint.

Enamored with the outside, your expectations are high walking in. You pause at the threshold and step inside the foyer. *Impressive,* is what comes to mind. The paint, the furnishings, and décor announce designer quality, but the surface conceals the home's dirty little secrets. Underneath the glowing hardwood and ornate rugs is an eroding foundation and faulty electrical wiring that is a fire waiting to happen. Peek behind the custom paint and wallpaper to find walls without insulation. The roof lacks proper support because building supplies were substituted with cheaper materials to save money. Load bearing walls are not properly placed nor are they comprised of the sturdy materials necessary to satisfy their purpose. What appears to be brilliantly made is subpar and won't withstand time. As life beats upon it, along with daily wear and tear, the dysfunction starts to show. But, that's not apparent now.

To meet the market demands, and also make a quick profit, the builder hurriedly threw it together. Less is more to him... less time, less contractors, less materials, less cost. He cuts corners, especially in areas where it won't be seen.

He distracts with aesthetics in hopes the poor quality will go unnoticed. People fall for it all the time. You fall for it, too.

A year later, the beautiful home that you couldn't wait to live in, starts to hint of its problems. The walls show cracks from settling and the kitchen fuse always blows. The utility bills are outrageous, but you blame it on the cold winter and unusually hot summer. The hardwood is raised in the back corner of the living room. You're not quite sure how you missed it.

Five years later, everywhere you look the faulty foundation makes itself known. Doors and windows won't open or close smoothly, more cracks appear, and the floor has departed far from level. The roof shifts from lack of support, and starts to slowly leak behind the ceiling plaster. Drip by drip until it's finally noticed, but only when the smooth surface of the ceiling starts to break away.

Beyond frustrated, you want out of this house! There is no way you can continue to live like this, with problem after problem. Every year it gets worse! You can't afford to stay in it anymore. You're afraid of what else will fall apart and what time will expose. What were once hidden troubles have become your primary focus. They refuse to hide behind the pretty paint and design.

Desperate to get out of this nightmare, you start to look for ways to be free. You soon realize, however, that you are not in a dream. It's reality, and the house is you. Built without thought of the blueprint, or care of the Master's plan, your life reflects the broken-down house.

Which leaves you to wonder, *what's the proper way to build the House of You?*

Chapter 1: The House of You

If a kingdom is divided against itself, that
kingdom cannot stand. If a house is divided
against itself, that house cannot stand.
Mark 3:24-25 (NIV)

If I asked you about your purpose in life, what would you say? Do you have any clue why you are here? What part do you play in God's plan? Do you yearn for something, but can't figure out what it is? Can you tell me what you're made of, your unique blend, which empowers you to achieve your calling...your destiny? If you lack answers to any of these questions, then read on. This book takes you through the structural components and recommends tools to help you discover your spiritual DNA.

To properly build the House of You and activate your God-given identity and destiny, only His supplied materials can be used. They are uniquely designed and individually assigned so your house will stand firm. Nevertheless, how you build your house is up to you. What you seek to learn, understand and apply, determines whether you sink or stand. It's your job to discover His exclusive design and the treasures hidden within you.

The core components are critical, and similar to the major structural elements when building a home. The way you're built determines how you function, as well as, stand up against the trials of this world. Any misappropriation or substitution, results in shifting and sway, with risk of collapse. It also affects the proper expression of your identity and calling.

Each of us is uniquely made and designed for a purpose that He planned for each of us before we were born. Though made of flesh, soul and spirit, the House of You is more than a body. It's a temple. It's the desired dwelling place of God, but it's also an instrument to be used for His glory while in this world. The House of You hosts riches of resources for a specific assignment and purpose. It's a storehouse of His gifts, talents and strengths individually wrapped by personality and identity. Our mission is to discover our identity in Christ, and live out our purpose and destiny ordained by the Master Builder.

So, what are these critical components required to wisely build the House of You? Individually they have specific uses within the body of Christ, but when operating together they complete the masterpiece of you. They are the support structures that reside under the roof of your God-given identity that work together to fulfill your destiny.

The House of You is built on:

- Relationship Foundation
- Spiritual Gifts

- Life Experiences
- Skills
- Strengths
- Talents
- Personality

The House of You

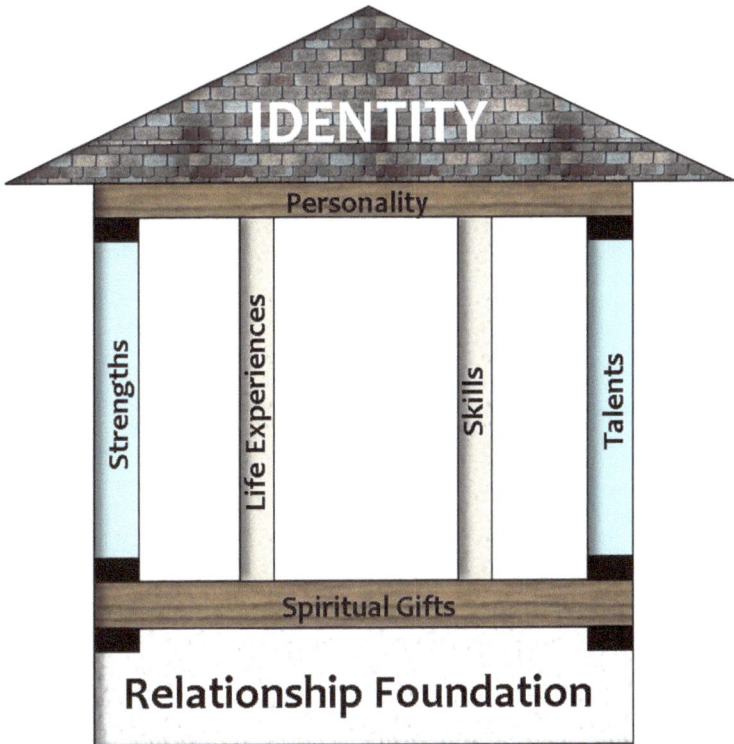

IDENTITY

Personality

Strengths

Life Experiences

Skills

Talents

Spiritual Gifts

Relationship Foundation

Figure 1: The House of You. Free worksheet download available at www.michellechudy.com

Chapter 2: The Foundation

"Anyone who listens to my teaching and follows it is wise, like a person who builds a house on solid rock. Though the rain comes in torrents and the floodwaters rise and the winds beat against that house, it won't collapse because it is built on bedrock. But anyone who hears my teaching and doesn't obey it is foolish, like a person who builds a house on sand. When the rains and floods come and the winds beat against that house, it will collapse with a mighty crash."
Matthew 7:24-27 (NLT)

A simple children's song echoes Jesus' words, "The wise man built his house upon a rock. The wise man built his house upon a rock. The wise man built his house upon a rock, and the rain came tumbling down. Oh, the rain came down and the floods came up. The rain came down and the floods came up. The rain came down and the floods came up, and the wise man's house stood firm."

Just ask any builder, the foundation is the most important part of the house. It bears the full load and secures the entire structure. It dictates the building's future because it's the anchor of everything that follows. That slab, which is never seen, can cost you greatly, if not built to the highest standards. *Isn't it just a slab of concrete and just a little mistake? Surely that ½" off square won't matter.* You rationalize that you can make adjustments as you go. But as you continue to build, making corrective actions, you realize that the ½" is contributing to a greater gap. Now it's apparent to everyone that the roof doesn't align. What is happening is referred to as compounding defects which means your mistakes grow as you continue to build. What started off small is exacerbated with each layer of construction. And no matter how hard you try to fix the symptoms, only the repair to the foundation will solve the problems. It then becomes the most expensive thing to repair because everything now rests upon it.

Your foundation is as equally important. What you choose to build your house upon will determine how you think, feel and act. It is the most important part of your temple, the House of You. So, what is this rock that the wise man built on? What is of the highest standard that will ensure your house won't come crashing down? That rock is Jesus Christ.

With Jesus who is the name above all names, and the highest standard you can find, you are building on a secure foundation. He must be the basis on which everything in your house is anchored. He provides the strength to support the load, and the level that guarantees alignment and proper construction. You'll never find a mistake in Him that leads to compounding defects. You're building on the only source of perfection that can't be found elsewhere. This foundation is poured when you enter into a relationship with Jesus Christ as your LORD and Savior.

If you were to inspect the House of You, what would you find as your foundation? Is it self? Career? Money? Family? Anything other than Jesus will distort your identity and shift you from your destiny. Nothing, and no one, is capable of supporting and encouraging the proper construction of you. So, are you the wise builder or a fool?

You can guarantee that your house will stand by calling on Jesus as LORD. Salvation is a free gift to all who believe and only requires childlike faith to receive. If you have never accepted Christ as your personal Lord and Savior, it is as simple as *ABC*. **A**dmit that Jesus Christ is God's Son. **B**elieve that He died for your sins, rose again, and is now seated at God the Father's right hand. **C**onfess that Jesus is your Savior and invite Him to be LORD of your life. It's through relationship with Jesus alone that a firm foundation is made. If you would like to ask Jesus to be your Savior, please pray the following prayer:

Dear Jesus,

You are the Christ! I confess that I'm a sinner. I believe You are the only one who can save me and give me eternal life. I believe You are God's only Son who died for my sins in my place, rose from the grave and now sit in heaven at God's right hand. I want a relationship with you and ask you to be LORD of my life. Please fill me with Your Holy Spirit, so I can live for You.

If you just prayed the prayer above, write today's date on your foundation. If you already knew Jesus as LORD and Savior, then write the date you entered into the salvation covenant with Him. Congratulations! Your foundation is perfect and ready to continue building the House of You!

YOUR FOUNDATION

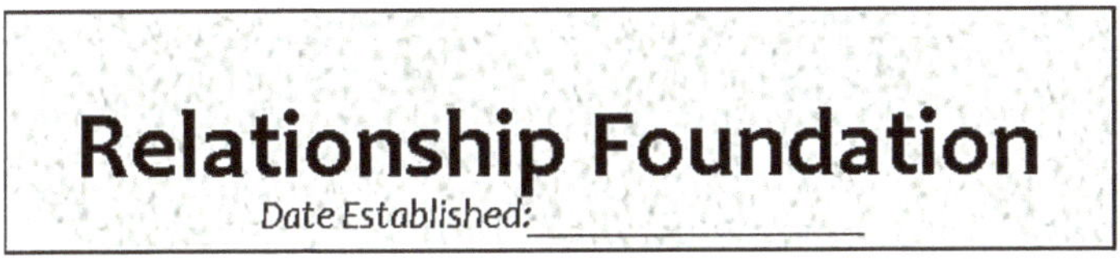
Relationship Foundation
Date Established:

Figure 2: The House of You Foundation

Chapter 3: Standing on Your Spiritual Gifts

For just as each of us has one body with many members, and these members do not all have the same function, so in Christ we, though many, form one body, and each member belongs to all the others. We have different gifts, according to the grace given to each of us. Romans 12:4-6a (NIV)

Layered on your relationship foundation is the investment or endowment God made in you, through His first gift to you, the Holy Spirit. As promised by Jesus before He ascended, you received the Holy Spirit when you accepted Christ as your Savior. The purpose of the Holy Spirit is to guide you in all truth, but also empower you to bring heaven to earth. One of the ways this is accomplished is through spiritual gifts.

These gifts are a supernatural grace, powered by the Spirit, to help you complete your mission as part of His church by equipping you. Your gifting also reveals clues to your purpose and function in the body of Christ. They can't be earned nor are they given based on individual ability. Your spiritual gift is free because of God's grace! The gifts were never intended for personal advancement, but to benefit others. Spiritual gifts manifest as natural and supernatural abilities.

To every Christ follower, He gave *at least one gift*, but it's often more than one. That means *no one is left out!* You will also never find one person with all of the gifts because we were meant to work together as the body of Christ. Not everyone can be the "eye" or the "foot". It takes all members (gifts) working together, for the body to function as a whole in how it was designed.

If you are a child of God, you have a spiritual gift, assigned specifically to you, that is part of your spiritual DNA. Do you know what your spiritual gifts are? You'll find multiple scriptural references to the gifts, but the key passages are in Romans 12, 1 Corinthians 12, Ephesians 4, and 1 Peter 4. The spiritual gifts are: *administration; apostleship; celibacy; discernment; evangelism; exhortation; faith; giving; healing; helps; hospitality; intercession; interpretation of tongues; knowledge; leadership; mercy; miracles; missionary; music; pastor/shepherd; prophecy; poverty; teaching; tongues; wisdom; and writing*.

People often find they have more than one, and have a gift mix. Some gifts are more prevalent than others, or clustered based on their intended use. The gift mix provides clues to your purpose and calling. For example, my gift mix is clustered. If I had to list my top three gifts, it would be in groups because I scored the same for multiple gifts, i.e. "clustered". My top gifts are wisdom and prophecy; secondary are faith, encouragement, knowledge, exhortation, and writing; and tertiary are leadership and pastoring. But it is to be also noted, that the scoring between my three clusters is marginal, which becomes apparent, when I flow from all three clusters.

Another revealing fact to God's purpose for you is the categories of your gifts. Spiritual gifts are diverse but fall into three major categories of: motivational; ministry; and manifestation. Your spiritual DNA and gift mix reveals how you will function within the body, and the categories often indicate how.

Take the time to find a good bible study on the spiritual gifts and how each is applied. This will provide deeper insight, and educate and equip you on how to use your gifts. By doing so, you will grow into your purpose and to step into your assigned place. By not operating in your gifts, you handicap the body of Christ because it's missing your vital piece of function that only you were designed to do.

To discover your spiritual gifts, seek the Lord and ask Him to reveal your gifts to you. You can also ask your church if they have a gift inventory, or you can go online and use one of the free assessment tools. If you choose the online option, search for "spiritual gift inventory", and you'll find multiple choices for your selection.

In the construction of your house below, list your top three spiritual gifts, which stand on the foundation of your relationship with Jesus. If your gifts are clustered, then write down the top three groups by stacking your gifts. Be sure to jot down any notes from your bible study on the gifts that apply to your mix and how they are used. These details will help reveal your purpose, calling and destiny.

YOUR SPIRITUAL GIFTS

My Spiritual Gifts

Relationship Foundation
Date Established:_____

Figure 3: The House of You Spiritual Gifts

Chapter 4: Life, Passions, Grief & Skills

And we know that God causes everything to work together for the good of those who love God and are called according to His purpose for them. Romans 8:28 (NLT)

How would you feel if I told you, you were framed? You really are! The person you are now is the result of the sum of your life experiences, passions, grief and skills. All these things help to frame who you are. Some were God-given, others acquired. But, He promises to work all things together for good, if you love Him and are called for His purpose. If you accepted Christ as your Savior, then that is you!

Life has a way of sweeping you along with its current, if you're not careful. Like it or not, it shapes who you are and provides subject-matter-expertise through on-the-job training. There is no one more qualified than the person who has experienced (insert topic here) in life. That topic can be whatever applies to your life...love, marriage, divorce, parenting, abuse, cancer, abortion, rape, success, etc. It's your testimony.

Your history forecasts your ministry because it gives you credibility, and a foundation to provide comfort and guidance to others. God also loves to take your worst nightmare and turn it into something good for Him. It's His beauty for your ashes. Another telltale sign of your destiny are your passions and what grieves you. What causes you the most joy and the most pain often indicates a call in those areas. He can use both good and bad experiences to open doors, all with the purpose to advance His kingdom on earth.

Prophetic words are also indicators that reveal pieces of His plan for you. Take note, it's imperative that you test the spirits before receiving the word and running with it. But, embrace the ones that the Holy Spirit confirms. These prophecies are meant to help you navigate the road of your destiny and give glimpses of your future. A prophetic word, along with your faith that's plugged into God, can call forth the unseen and the promises of God into existence. It's an act of spiritual warfare.

Got skills? Your skills are an area of expertise or a particular ability that you do well. These can be inherent or learned, and are a kingdom asset to list for the House of You. There are many references throughout the Bible of God giving skills to His people. In Exodus 35, He filled the workers who were building the temple with skills to do the work of engravers, designers and embroiderers. To Daniel (Belteshazzar), Hananiah (Shadrach), Mishael (Meshach) and Azariah (Abednego), God gave them skill in all literature and wisdom. Daniel and his friends excelled in Babylonian captivity even though they were slaves. Joseph was skilled at interpreting dreams and management, and landed a job as second in command under Pharaoh, before he was released from prison!

Skills can also be acquired through education, training and practice. Can you cook well? Then it is a skill that can be used for good. Do you play the piano or sing? It's a skill for His good and His glory. How about skills at making money, managing people, working with children or turning a wrench? There is nothing too great or too small that is off limits to God, and can also reveal His purpose for you.

So, let's frame out the House of You! Take a few minutes to pray and think about your life. Ask the Holy Spirit to reveal your framework. On the left side of your house by life experiences, write down the areas that helped shape you. Don't be afraid to list the bad along with the good. Here's a hint...if it caused you great shame, then it is typically an area God wants to use for ministry. What better thing is there, than to turn the table on the devil's plan to destroy you. Also, be sure to list your passions, areas of grief, and any relevant prophetic word.

Next, inventory your skill sets and jot down any ability that you do really well on the right side of your house. Don't discount your skills! Remember how they were used by the temple workers, Daniel and Joseph, just to name a few. By the looks of it, your house is going to be glorious!

Life Experiences

Skills

My Spiritual Gifts

Relationship Foundation
Date Established:_____

Figure 4: The House of You Frame

Chapter 5: Strengths & Talents

Each one should test their own actions. Then they can take pride in themselves alone, without comparing themselves to someone else, for each one should carry their own load. Galatians 6:4-5 (NIV)

If you want to test your strength, then see how long you can stand under a load. The load can be physical, emotional or spiritual, but is always heavy. Used to stabilize a structure and sustain the weight, a load-bearing wall must be made of sturdy stuff which is often concrete, brick or block. It holds up everything above and conducts the weight to the foundation. Messing with a load-bearing wall not only affects stability, it can be disastrous.

You, too, have load bearing capabilities that stem from your strengths and talents. God made you with a unique set of talents that converge into strength themes. Just like a snowflake, no two people manifest their strengths in the same way. Your strengths not only make you stand out in a crowd, but are areas where you are highly productive and confident.

So, what's the difference between a talent and strength? According to Gallup, a strength is the ability to consistently provide near-perfect performance in a specific activity. Talents are naturally recurring patterns of thought, feeling, or behavior that can be productively applied. Talents, knowledge, and skills – along with time spent (i.e., investment) practicing, developing your skills, and building your knowledge base – combine to create your strengths.

Not long ago, there was a rampant trend to identify and train up a person's weaknesses. The thought was to make a person balanced and strong in all areas, resulting in higher productivity. I'm sure I'm not the only one who found this depressing and defeating. Especially in the business world, weaknesses were not deemed flaunt-worthy.

Thanks to one of my corporate life experiences, the strengths and talents area of the House of You was unlocked through a professional development exercise. *It was energizing!* Finally, there was someone or something that understood me and nailed me with accuracy.

Along with my coworkers, I took the **StrengthsFinder 2.0** assessment and was blown away with the results. It analyzed my dominant talents and identified my strength themes. And if that were not enough, it summarized how my strength themes manifested in me. It told me areas where I would stand out and what would shut me down. By far, it was the best professional and personal tool I had ever encountered. There were so many applications for the results it was mind boggling. From organizational planning to project partnering, even to creating a positive atmosphere in my home, when you operate in your strength themes, you excel!

So how does this apply to the House of You? Your strength themes partnered with your spiritual gifts are not only complementary, but powerful! They help to release the supernatural flow that God created in you. StrengthsFinder themes help you to find or eliminate your place of ministry within the body. It helps you to better understand the way that God made you and gives you opportunity to leverage your best, for His glory.

Let me share my Top 5 Themes and show how they help me function. According to my assessment, I'm an *activator; relator; strategic; achiever; and responsibility*. My top strength as activator indicates I'm a doer and can turn thoughts into action. My insights summary describes how I manifest the activator strength through candid communication, and strive to energize others. I empower people with my confidence. I'm straightforward, edifying, a motivator, an improver, confident and I get stuff done! This in mind, coupled with my spiritual gift mix inventory that shows I rank high in speaking motivational gifts, I can narrow my purpose for the kingdom. My gifts and strengths manifest through my writing, speaking, mentoring, and coaching.

Now, back to the House of You for the next round of construction! Pray and ask the Holy Spirit to reveal your hidden strengths and talents. To help with this endeavor, I unabashedly recommend you take the Clifton's **StrengthsFinder 2.0** assessment authored by Tom Rath to identify your strength themes. It's a small price for the value of the insights. You can find it in most book stores, normally in the business section, or order it online. Once you purchase the book, you'll receive an access code to take the online assessment. Once you complete the assessment, list your Top 5 Strength Themes and any additional talent the Holy Spirit Reveals.

YOUR STRENGTHS & TALENTS

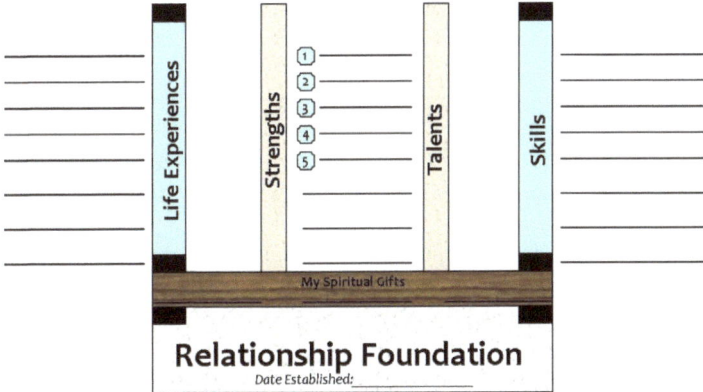

Figure 5: The House of You Load

Chapter 6: Personality

So, how does it make you feel knowing that God is responsible for the making of your personality? For some that's comforting, and to others they may wonder, *what was He thinking?!* For me, it was comforting and confounding.

Personality defined is a sum of a combination of characteristics or qualities that form your distinctive self. It filters and expresses everything that is packed inside of you. It stamps your gifts with your bent, your skills with your brand, and your strengths and talents with your flare. Your personality is you, and there is no way around it.

When trying to find your place and purpose in His kingdom, personality with the aforementioned components, can point the way. I've heard many preachers say how Paul's dominant personality would have torn up the church, if he was permitted to remain past the church plant. God moved Paul on, as Timothy the encourager was called in to build up the body. Both personalities were critically needed, but each had distinctive purpose and seasons.

What do you know about your personality? Do you know if you are dominant or compliant? Are you sanguine or melancholy, or maybe an ENTJ? There many labels depending on the test. I've seemed to acquire tags from most, thanks to my military and corporate careers. According to the DISC, I'm dominant. Briggs Myers said I'm ENTJ. The Four Temperaments say I'm choleric with a lot of sanguine and support my all or nothing behaviors. The one I like the most was the Predictive Index; whose summary was like reading my biography. Let me be clear, I'm not advocating the labels, but the gleaning of the insights.

Your personality indicates how you relate to people and different environments. You can use the testing and assessment information to hone your kingdom fit. You can eliminate or validate based on what you find. I believe it was Charles Stanley who penned prophets are like a strong spice. A little goes a long way! Based on that analogy, you can surmise that prophets typically have a strong personality. Well, guess what? My top spiritual gift is prophecy, and I have a dominant personality! See the connection? Everything starts to tick and tie when you look at your structural components and see how they filter through personality into your identity.

So, let's go back to the House of You and install the ceiling joist of personality. Always pray and ask the Holy Spirit to guide your research and lead you into truth. Go to the internet and search for "free personality test" and multiple assessment options will appear in the search results. I don't believe that one test has all of the answers, but I do prefer some over others because they are more robust.

I recommend that you take more than one. They are *FREE*! Each assessment tool gives a different slant or insight on how your personality manifests in various situations. When you answer the questions truthfully, and not what you think you should say or do, the results are pretty accurate. Take as many as you can and print off the results. Study the summaries and pull out the key words or statements that resonate with your spirit. Look at the environments mentioned and how you interact with people. Highlight how you interact with people. One thing I know for sure, people are important to Jesus. He died for them. You can bet your purpose for His kingdom involves people, too.

When you've completed your personality test, enter it into the House of You. Add any relevant insights that you pulled from your assessments. Your house is almost complete!

Personality Type:

Life Experiences

Strengths

① ——————
② ——————
③ ——————
④ ——————
⑤ ——————

——————
——————

Talents

Skills

My Spiritual Gifts

Relationship Foundation
Date Established:_____

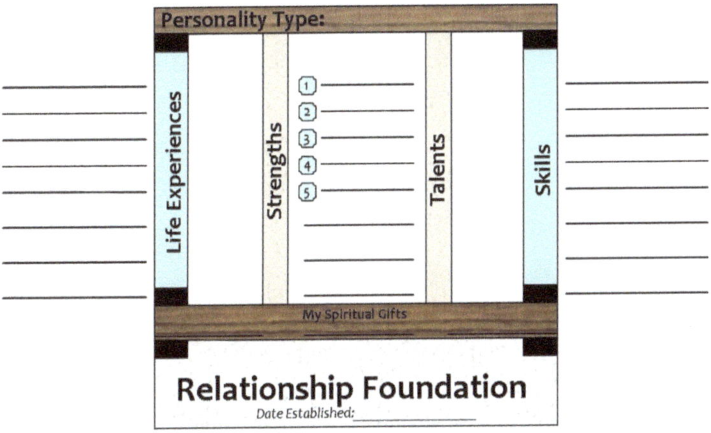

Figure 6: The House of You Personality

Chapter 7: Identity

How would you describe your identity? Is it your title, gender or your name? Do you have a collection of other people's answers, who told you who you are, and now you are trying to live up to those labels? Or have you ascribed to your own answers based on who and what you want to be? What's your truth?

Identity defined is the fact of being who or what a person is. The quandary comes when you really don't know who or what you are. But that can be easily solved when you know Christ because He tells you who you are. To embrace and walk in your authentic identity comes down to a pair of eyes. How you see yourself determines if you are an imposter in your own skin or living as your authentic self.

When it comes to the House of You, you can have every other component in place and lose the benefits of it with the roofing of a skewed identity. No matter how well the rest of the house is built, a roof aligned incorrectly is a liability to the entire house. Your identity is your covering and ensures that you bring everything underneath into manifested fullness.

Take some time and reflect on your identity. Write down around your roof what **you** say is your identity.

Figure 7: The House of You Identity

So, how's your vision? Are you able to see who you really are? If you see your identity through eyes other than His, then you are visually impaired. That includes your own eyes. To know your true identity, it comes from Christ's eyes alone and how He sees you. He created you and knows for a fact who and what you are. What does He see?

Go to God's word for your truth. Search for a study or teaching on identity in Christ and see who He says that you are. When you are finished with you research, write your discoveries beside of your properly installed roof. And while you're at in, go back to the first roof and cross through the ones that are false. Better yet, write the name of Jesus over each false identity because when God the Father looks at you, He only sees Jesus.

The House of _____

(Print your name)

Properly Built & Installed by Jesus Christ!

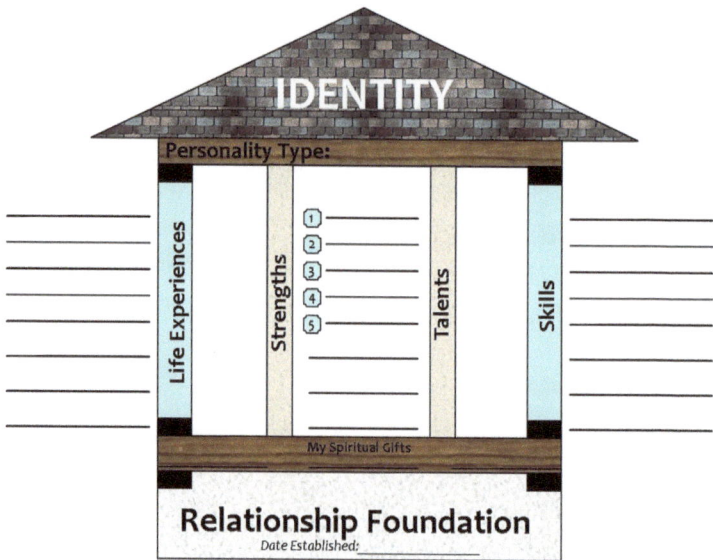

Figure 8: The House of You. Free worksheet download available at www.michellechudy.com

Chapter 8: Powered by Love

Jesus replied, "'You must love the LORD your God with all your heart, all your soul, and all your mind.' This is the first and greatest commandment. A second is equally important: 'Love your neighbor as yourself.' The entire law and all the demands of the prophets are based on these two commandments." Matthew 22:37-40 (NLT)

What powers your house? Now that your house is gloriously built, it beckons for life to move in and transform it into a home. How will people know that your house is His house, built for His purpose and structured for His plan? Unless the lights are turned on, it appears lifeless and vacant. You require a power source to make your light shine.

Just like today's many energy sources, the House of You can be powered from many options...selfishness, carnality, greed, envy, success, etc. But according to Jesus, there is only one indicator that proves you are sourced by Him. Love is the indicator of God's presence in your life. Jesus is the only reason why we can love one another, and it's because He first loved us. His disciples are known by their love. And according to the two greatest commandments, everything hinges on love. So, ask yourself this question, *have I learned how to love?* Better yet ask yourself, *how do I love?*

As part of your spiritual DNA, you have your own way of expressing and receiving love. The agony comes when there is a disconnect from giver to receiver. Unless you understand how you express love, and how the person you love on is made to feel loved, you can both wither from a frustrated and loveless environment. Like a shade loving plant unfortunately placed in a sunny garden, it shrivels up and dies. Or consider a newborn who fails to thrive even though they are fed milk. The baby is getting milk, but for whatever reason the baby isn't able to receive the proper nutrients needed to sustain life. No matter how much milk the baby drinks, the baby doesn't benefit because it lacks what the baby really needs. That's what it is like when you need love delivered through words, but it's expressed via a hug. The hug means nothing to you because you only receive love's nutrients through words and not touch.

Communication of love is vital, and that's exactly what it is, a communication. As we pursue our unique spiritual blend and learn *how* to love, identification of our method of love delivery is crucial. It expresses the very nature and essence of Christ and through it we give and receive life.

So, what is love's communication method? Simply put, it's language. Language expresses words or thoughts in both verbal and non-verbal ways. It is the delivery mechanism that ushers in understanding between the one "speaking" and the other "hearing".

In *The 5 Love Languages: The Secret to Love that Lasts*, Dr. Gary Chapman identified five languages of how love is communicated: *words of affirmation; acts of service; receiving gifts; physical touch; and quality time*. He also suggests that people often have a primary and secondary language to express and receive love. But in order to love well as we are commanded to, it's important to understand all five. Love is so important to Jesus it begs we become multilingual. By not just knowing our own languages, we are able to express love to others in the ways they receive it best.

It's time to let the love light shine in the House of You! If you know your primary and secondary love languages, write them under the appropriate light in your house. If you're not sure how you communicate and receive love, ask the Holy Spirit what they are. You can also go online and take the free 5 Love Languages quiz offered by Dr. Chapman. Just search for "five love languages".

When taking the quiz, it is really important to answer the questions as honestly as possible. Don't answer based on what you think you should say or what you've been told is best. Answer what is most meaningful to *you*. You'll only discover your truth when you answer for you.

Let me give you a quick example from one of my coaching clients. For years this person thought their primary love language was quality time because of how she was raised. She learned that time was an expression of love, and was told that she should feel loved because she received a lot of quality time. Because of her love and honor for her parent, she adopted quality time as a love language and suppressed her own. Upon retaking the quiz, she discovered that her true love languages are acts of service and words of affirmation! Can you imagine the frustration of trying to feel loved when her husband attempted to "speak her language" only to feel unloved? Or the burden of trying to communicate through quality time, when she oozes love through her acts and words? It's liberating to love in how God designed you to flow!

As you discover your love languages, I encourage you to bring others into knowledge of theirs. If you are married or have children, then it is especially valuable to understand each one's frame of reference for love. Take the time to study each other's love languages and learn how to minister to each other with the greatest gift you can give. "Three things will last forever – faith, hope, and love – and the greatest of these is love" (1Corinthians 13:13 NLT). A life lived well is a life that loves. And they will know you are His disciples by your love for one another. Speak love, be His love, arise and shine!

The Love Powered House of

_____

(Print your name)

Properly Built, Installed &

Powered by Jesus Christ!

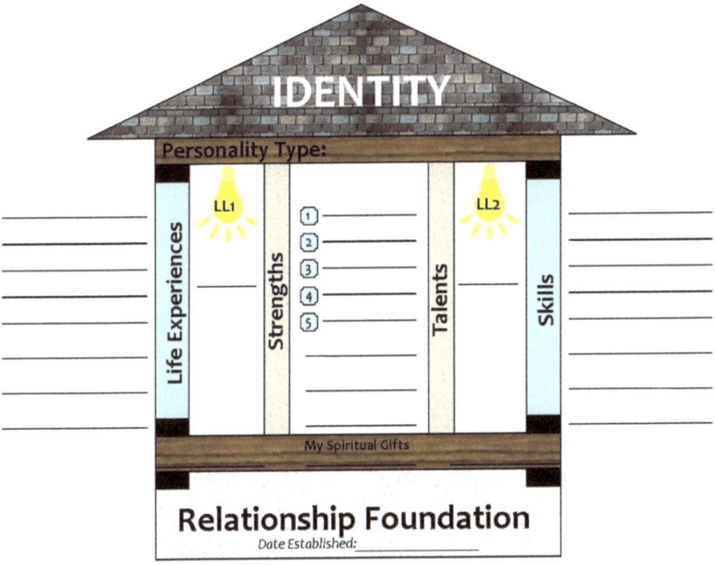

Figure 9: The House of You Love Languages.
Free worksheet download available at www.michellechudy.com

Personal Notes

Personal Notes

Personal Notes

Personal Notes

Afterword

Congratulations on your beautiful home that is designed and built by the Master Builder! I told you it would be glorious. Now that you are settling in, you can rest in knowing that you are built for His purpose and structured for His plan. The enigma of destiny will start to unfold.

Can I give you destiny specifics or key traits to unlock your future? Sorry, but no. I think we all wish that we came with an instruction manual or a blueprint of our design. But, I think we both know that would take all of the faith out of it, and the thrill of discovery. Our search requires seeking Him, and He enjoys our company.

To find His purpose and plan for you, you can use your construction list from the House of You to eliminate what you're not. You can use the knowledge and insights from your spiritual DNA to position yourself in the proper environments for you to thrive. Never forget that you are the only one who can meet the kingdom need with the components He placed only in you.

About the Author

Michelle Chudy helps unfulfilled believers discover their God-given identity so they can walk the path of destiny. She is like an investigator who solves the case of you!

Her mission or "why" is to equip the saints. Michelle helps people discover their authentic, God-given self so they can be empowered in their calling, flow in their gifts and strengths, and live the purpose God designed only for them. Michelle's life coaching career began in 2008, and she has helped numerous clients overcome hindrances and live empowered lives through Christ.

Michelle is an author, speaker and certified business and life coach. She applies her dynamic approach through integrated coaching with transformational solutions to both individual and business clients alike. She is a facilitator of change that results in on-target growth.

- Author of *The House of You Series*, *Song of the Barren: Miscarriages to Miracles*, and *The Battle of Surrender: One Woman's Journey to Sacrifice*
- Empowered Living & Identity Mapping Expert
- Certified Business Coach and Academy Trainer
- Seasoned Marketing Executive and Business Innovator
- Dynamic Encouragement Speaker on Identity, Purpose, Destiny & Personal Discovery

Author's Note

Did you enjoy *The House of You: Built for a Purpose. Structured for His Plan?* Please take time to leave a review on Amazon and applicable sites. Your review is welcome and greatly appreciated! Help to build the kingdom by equipping the saints with tools from *The House of You Series*. Tell your friends how *The House of You: Built for a Purpose. Structured for His Plan.* helped to edify you and share it with them.

God Bless,

Michelle

To learn more about Michelle and her writings follow her on www.michellechudy.com, FaceBook, Instagram and Twitter. To purchase her autobiography of *The Battle of Surrender: One Woman's Journey to Sacrifice* or *Song of the Barren: Miscarriages to Miracles* shop the store at www.michellechudy.com or any other online book retailer where available.

Endnotes

[1]Gallup, What is the difference between a talent and a strength?
http://strengths.gallup.com/help/general/125543/difference-talent-strength.aspx

www.ingramcontent.com/pod-product-compliance
Lightning Source LLC
LaVergne TN
LVHW010023070426
835508LV00001B/23